WHAT BRINGS YOU HERE SO LATE?

WHAT BRINGS YOU HERE SO LATE?

A Poem

Tony Conran

First published in 2008

ISBN: 978-1-84527-170-1

Published with the financial support of the Welsh Books Council

Book designed by Alan McPherson

Published by
Gwasg Carreg Gwalch,
12 Iard yr Orsaf, Llanrwst, Wales, LL26 0EH.
Tel: 01492 642031 Fax: 01492 641502
e-mail: llyfrau@carreg-gwalch. com
www. carreg-gwalch. com

Printed and published in Wales.

CONTENTS

for my daughters

ONE

'What brings you here so late?' said the knight on the road.
'I gc to meet my God,' said the child as he stood.
And he stood, and he stood, and 'twere well he stood.
'I go to meet my God,' said the child as he stood.

'How will you go by land?' said the knight on the road.
'With a strong staff in my hand,' said the child as he stood.
And he stood, and he stood, and 'twere well he stood.
'With a strong staff in my hand,' said the child as he stood.

'How will you go by sea?' said the knight on the road.
'With a good ship under me,' said the child as he stood.
And he stood, and he stood, and 'twere well he stood.
'With a good ship under me,' said the child as he stood ...

from the singing of Frank Quinn, Co. Tyrone

Chapter 1. LEOPARD

In the toffee-paper ivy
Where the Martian boys threatened
Each other like cobras –

I was a leader, intellect,
Icon of their own distinctness.
Leopard asleep in a tree.

I was the story they lived in
Before I hatched
Or heard my crumpled voice.

I have guilt from that time:
James, poor tall simpleton
Sucked at by whirling satchels, bullied,

(And I knew him for human
Even before I knew myself).
'Barrabas,' I shouted, mobbing like birds.

That was only one story.
The thrushes of Dinerth,
Bear-fortress, my sacred hill –

Ochre and lime. Caves hot with urine.
Sloe bushes on the thin turf.
The ruins of Llys Euryn, Plum Hall,

Where three damson trees stuck it out still
Over the lintel,
And the enormous quarry beetled down

To newt ponds in the debris ...
There were stories there
Where the leopard hung.

★

And the shores, with their curdling rivers,
Flatrocks and dusty shingle
When the visitors packed for home –

Land between the two piers
With its long fingers of light
Ruffling the strand.

I'd been a child there, pushing the sand
Into castles, tunnelling the wetness
For dinky-car roads. For canals.

The other reality of me –
A grown-up's vision, puny, pitiable,
But dear. Something to be helped

Or not to be helped. A boy built wrong
That had to be hedged with splints,
With excuses. Poor love ...

★

Came a day when the leopard went for a walk in the woods
Swishing his tail, the dappling of the sunlit leaf
Sometimes hiding all but the intensity of his eyes –

The black hunger of his mind. Where were they,
All the boys that lived in his story? Girls
Flickered between visions, flirted like goldfinches.

So he made them tales. Of the nape of their necks
Layered with curls. Of their eyes –
The safe, dainty mockery in them. Of bare feet,

Bare arms, bare anything ... He was happy.
A caged big cat in the sun. Poor love
Creeping closer to consciousness, like a beggar.

*

Boys would kiss and tell.
Odysseys of mistaken intentions,
Scilla and Charybdis.

I was all ears. Like a spaniel
I padded after their amours,
I sniffed at meanings.

I was a base-camp for their Everest.
Inventions drifted like blizzards
Through the changed faces.

And the girls' subterranean
Expectancy echoed
In the mind

Like a river,
A frozen waterfall
Or the swarming of bees.

*

In the landscaped park where a Calvary
Croes-yn-Eirias
Once stood

Philip went walking with me –

Foot light as a squirrel,
A body that had wit in itself
Like a tune, a shape of gracenotes,

He delighted me. Like a tomcat
I watched the antics of a little queen.
Time contracted to where he was.

I could not say I loved him
Or that I wanted to touch him –
Still less to kiss his lips.

There is a pre-love kind of loving,
A falling in love
Before you notice it.

And it did not last. Our friendship
Faltered, or he moved away.
That year, we were strangers again.

After that, I only saw him once
On my twentieth birthday
In a dream.

*

Down a great concourse, in the gloom
I trod the steps of death
And Philip below me, visible.

Certain veiled old women
Moving between the shades
Comforted us.

Cut. And God like a business executive
At a great desk
In the sunlight

Rejecting Philip. Me, though, he gentled.
Red angels undressed me,
Took me through a door to heaven.

Cut. God again. I looked down. I was covered with huge warts.
He came over to me, casually broke one off,
They disappeared.

Me trying to talk. Guilt. And thirst
Like the mariner's, like biting a sloe.
I could not speak.

God pouring water into a glass,
Offered it me.
It was like waking up. I woke up.

The angels undressed me to my vest.
'When next you come,' said God,
'Everything you've done

Will be judged.'

Chapter 2. UNFINISHED SYMPHONY

Staying with my aunt in Mossley Hill
I walked back by the dark church
Between dusty toddlers in the field

Along Old Red Sandstone walls
Flaking, incised with soot,
To this particular sitting-room smell

And my aunt coming in from her ironing
To change the blue Columbia 78's
Over and over ...

Poor love hears it, the tune,
The three-four rhythm
– So – on the cellos ...

'Listen,' they say, 'I command you,
I am beautiful. We speak
To you.'

No one before now
Made me listen like this.
Poor love, poor love

Wants nothing
But the pain
Over and over

Of knowing this joy ...

That afternoon, that lifetime,
In my aunt's home
The *Unfinished* was vision –

Quod visum, placet:
That which, once it is seen,
Delights.

My own self
I listened to –

Understood
Beyond understanding

Schubert acknowledging me
And what I must die for.

Chapter 3. PARENTS

The war was over. Father could come
And poor love like a chrysalis
Unwrap, good boy, good boy,
Me, to man's estate.

Hiroshima. From India
Mother could come. On the platform
Her arms up, screaming my name.
Poor love had a lover now.

Poor love walked with her in the meadows
At the side of beechwoods,
Along chalkpits
Cracking brown flints under foot.

Talking, talking –
Poor love was a foreign country,
A grand tour,
A picture gallery, a chest of memories.

Poor love was like her own half-life,
Her intelligence –
She a student again,
Poor love her weekday assignment.

⋆

But the marriage arched above me, out of sight.
I hid from it as from the eye of God,
A kindly, sabbath world where my father
Precisely every least threepence
Entered, like a churchwarden. Where time
Was measured like a problem in Euclid,
Arrivals and departures at a station platform.

Where my mother admired him, grieved for
His trailing failure that was the shadow
Of their happiness together. My mother,
For all her ailments, her intimations
Of tragedy, was a success story,
A memsahib fraught with the Raj.
Without a qualm she sacrificed
Her smaller successes. Wasn't my father himself
A prime achievement? To keep him
Was worth her championship Bridge,
Her independence teaching science. Was it
(Though I never thought it then)
Worth being with her child?

⋆

High Wycombe ...

When we came here, my father went leopard-shooting.
I felt like a gipsy, camping
With my mother
In the tall eighteenth century house.

'Ho,' said my father, 'you don't need these toys any longer.'
A boy of sixteen – what's he need teddybears for?
Red Indians, or a farmyard of tin pigs,
The gravel population of a child?

And we rummaged through them, like a dream
Disinfecting them of me.
My spiralling heart would not reach home to them,
Those stations of my hands were shut.

'Ho,' said my father, 'we've no room for all your books.'
And the leopard obediently came down from his perch
In the mahogany tree
And lolloped over the veld.

Bang! bang! went my father. But poor love
Not having a visible childhood any longer
Curled round my mother's feet, pleading lost causes
With a forked tongue

Like a snake in Eden.

Chapter 4. FRESHER

Last autumn
I'd come to Bangor.
I was hermit
Knowing no one –
Conquistador
Free and exultant
In the heart's
El Dorado.

In my hermitage
Of streets and green hills
Intelligence
Was visionary.
Patterns in the loneliness
Were etched with light.

The wings' outgoing sweep
Of an intellect
Finding its country –
The long privation
Over, the bitter sea
Of the trivial
Overflown

And the white coral beaches
Young to my feet ...

*

The first of my poems came to me:

> *'Come,'* she commanded,
> *'Twine your speech –*
> *Your words can clothe me.*

I am cold
And naked to be born.
My flesh is white.

Give me green words
And a strange locality
To dye
My unborn whiteness

With the leaf
And pastoral homesteads
Of a name'.

Was it my twin
Peered up at me

Enticing me back
Where the foetus
Grew upstart
When the womb's
Cracked geology
Was new?

*

Patterns in the loneliness
Were etched with light.

The imperative of a poem –
Crannies of darkness.

Intelligence
Was visionary.

The unknowing of a poem –
Stupidity, frustration.

But still Pied Piper
Knew his way:

Echoes of rock
Counterpointed his flute.
The river's in flood.

His tunes
Wove in and out

Fleshing new stars,
Flowers to the root.

My hermitage
Of streets and green hills –

Impotence at my sleeve
Like a propositioning slut.

Chapter 5. SPEECH

I walked along the Embankment
In the wide wilderness
To St Thomas's.

Woolly tigers, boxes of bricks,
Alphabets, pop-guns
Piled one wall.

My speech therapist
Asked me,

    'Have you ever
Heard you talk?'

What, inside my head –
Conversations, intimacies, harangues
Like anyone else?

'I'm going to record you. You write,
Don't you? Tell me about that.
I've a friend who writes ...'

I told her my poetry story –
How, in the Goddess dark,
I find poems ...

'Right. Playback.'
Whirring tape, clattering dials.
'Now.'

Round me the sudden, luminous egg
Arched in menace.
World was hatching me.

I could hear voices from outside,
Could hear her voice, thickened
By the tape ...

'I've a friend who writes ...'
I braced myself
To listen to my story –

*

All I could hear ...

Odd clicks, whines, whisperings
And boom – boom – boom –
Like a lowing cow, urgent

As the bull calf I was to remember
In a tiny field
of milk-fragrant Logdal
Lorn from his herd, lonely
(As Erik said) for the ladies'
Sweet eyes and white haunches –

The tragedy of his maleness
In his bowels
For the first time

Good for nothing now
But the bone-saw and cleaver ...

Crying my bull protest,
A male weanling
In the night.

To this day I cannot
Understand myself on tape.

Chapter 6. CHEMISTRY

The leopard perched on the stairs
Reading. His ears flicked.
He made notes with his tail.

He walked in the sparse winter woodland
Of the elements. In the green sunlight
Of their courtship.

Androgenous hydrogen, like a baby Tiresias,
Its singularity beyond gender. How lightly
It cavorted in acid and base!

How obliging it stooged for us, for carbon
That virtuoso conjurer. Life
Wasn't its idea – but it helped, it helped!

And the great castrati, the noble gases,
Helium child of the sun, argon the traveller –
Sons of the morning, they shouted together.

Then those spluttering passionate creatures,
Sodium, potassium, so eager for love
They flustered cold air with their fire.

Perhaps only in flame were themselves –
Daffodil, violet ... The ionic world
Hid them, like mermaids alive only in brine.

And their dark compatriots of passion
The salt-begetters – fluorine that bites through glass,
So quick and phallic, rapes and is lost –

Chlorine the green man – the old roué
Bromine – iodine ... poison
Or vivificant, maleness like a scent of fox.

Sprawled on the turn of the stairs, the leopard
Crouched, watching the gods. He walked
In the thin upland scrub of an ancient book.*

Olympians, glimpsed in the glades. Bismuth,
Beryllium, cobalt, gold. Each one
To be known as a piece of music,

All its quirks and key-structures,
And the love-life in its compounds
Fabled, notated. Like a dance.

The leopard moved in their company
Like an acolyte. He wanted to touch
Even their abstraction.

I dared the last chapter: apocalypse,
Revelation according to Mendeléef.
The chiming of the gods.

Tribes of the elements, eight by eight,
Enacting, like number itself,
An exact yet fanciful eternity.

I was Pythagoras, opening
To the order of the spheres.
I answered the Sphinx.

No vision since
Has claimed such wonder,
Such allegiance from me.

Such comradeship with god.

* *Modern Inorganic Chemistry*, J.W. Mellor, D.Sc. 1914. All the science I had as a boy came from pre-1918 textbooks and an encyclopaedia of 1904.

*

Since that vision blazed
In a nineteenth century sky
Fifty years had passed –
Fifty light-years!

But already, even as the crouching leopard
On the stairs watched,
Those ancient books
Foretold its end.

All was not well with the immortals.
Time was besetting them.
One after another
Theogonies were falling.

Time streams in the rocks.
Hungry generations of stone
Through volcano and lifted seas
Crowded into the air.

Time. Evolution bore away
Archaeopterix and mammoth,
Dallied with the youth of apes
And made us.

Time. The skies exploded.
Galaxies and planets
Were historical
Like floodtide and ebb.

And now the bomb at Hiroshima
Gathered the elements
Like scum in Time's ladle.
Fifty years crashed to the ground.

The last of the immortals left the world.

★

The death of Alcestis.

I watched Apollo from my hermitage
Striding to and fro along the barbican
Of the palace at Pherae.
The god was nervous. Death in the vicinity
Crumpled his shadow on the stone.

These were people he loved, he owed love to,
And he an immortal. And yet
The Greek words that I puzzled over
– Balancing yets and buts,
On the one hand this, and on the other –
The words of the god before the gates at Pherae

'So now she lies inside there, propped
In their arms, near her end.
She must die, must leave them.
Today she must go. And I too
Must leave this house, which I so dearly love,
To avoid the taint of death ...'

So the immortal. And our mortality, the smell of it,
Was a tabu to him, a taken for granted sanctity
He could not trespass on
Even for love.

No wonder that in my hermitage
Of streets and green hills
Facing Hiroshima
The immortals left me –

I had only time, and the unclean comfort
Of the dying
To make them stay.

*

The Republic.

I walk the harbour streets, through the warehouses
Gay with bunting
For the festival. Young men from the shadows
Bar my way. 'No, Socrates,' they plead,
'You're not going yet. You're such a rare
Visitor. We're not all bills of lading,
Shipments of oil
Or slaves to the islands!'

Well, I know that. Clattering
Of their ideas seethes round me, plops and bumps
And reverberates in great smoking bubbles.

'And besides,' they say, 'you've not seen
Our pièce-de-résistance – tonight's
Chariot race with torches
In honour of the god ...'

Fires smoke and scar. Relay on relay
Charioteers swerve down the sky.
The young men talk of justice.

And the hunger drives us
As all imitate
What's eternity to each ...

Time's mimicry like a child
Yearning
For acknowledgement,

For praise.

*

Plato's Cave.

I had my back to the cliff-face, craning my neck
To find foothold. Heelblock. Or
Crack for the side of my sole.
I was hung from fingers reaching behind me
To the naked wall.

The cliff was like an anthill, swarming
With bodies, each about its business,
Up, down, avoiding
Or meeting; helping others to climb
Or treading them under.
All, except me, faced into the rock.

It was the cavern of time that I was in,
Plato's great cave –
Appetitive mankind prospecting
For brightnesses
Where the dull quartz
Caught light.

Spreadeagled against the rock,
Hardly able to shift,
I looked towards the opening of the cave.
'Who in eternity,' I thought, 'if I cried
Would hear me?'

Yet knowing that my eyes were sucked out
To that gap in the stone,
I had no home in the cave of time,
No fellow.
Perhaps too much a child

Clinging, frightened to grow up,
To follow my nose to my wants
Along a facing rock ...

Where all the eternals I belonged to
Were gone lost.

Chapter 7. MARGARET

Day and night hardly followed
In orderly fashion.
Lightnings brooded
On the horizon of time.
The small hours opened like trumpets.

We did not always know him. Strangers
In street or bazaar
Would have his eyes, his voice.
Outside town, we'd make a fire
By a wadi, and he'd be cooking for us.

And then, suddenly, here we are
At the ending of things –
A man in the distance of history
Lifted from the earth
Till a cloud hides him.

'People of Galilee,' say
The two quiet gentlemen in white,
'Why do you stand here
Staring into heaven?'
Cut. We disperse without trouble.

*

The God-Cycle?

John, supposing you're right
And the eternals are in love
With Time. God makes

Worlds for Christmas presents,
Valentine cards.
It's the thought that counts.

But the thought of God
Is God. Interfused
With time like body and soul

But beginning with a girl
Saying yes, in the half light
Between the created and the incarnate,

A single cell of her body
To be wrapped in the present
Of God to God –

A theology of Ascension.
The waters say of the world
– Sex, stone, birth, death –

You must be washed with fire.
It is the flickering, like a dream
At the end of time

Where the benatured God
Recovers for his love
His own benaturing gift.

*

A theology of love
Beginning with a girl
Saying yes, in the half light ...

My hermitage suddenly
A field full of folk –

I stumbled from the wood
With a single pale-tailed bluebell
Nodding in my fingers. How she laughed,
That crane of a girl!

And so
My schubertiads began –
Oddity and poems and traipsing
Over the shores. Talking
From street to digs, digs
To street again, sometimes
All night. Singing the Dies irae
In open-air gents
Under the moon.

*

To Beryl, her kindliness,
Merle, her kisses,
Nonn, the leap of her hair
Walking ...

Love at every café corner
In a mist of friendship
Loomed, in and out of absurdity
Like an otter playing
Hide and seek in a beck.

And always the theology
Of love, poor love – God
As small as a child,
As a mite,
As a mustard seed ...
The suffering servant,
The holy fool.

Troubadour in me
From hall to hall
Cursed and dreamt.
Childe Tony
To the dark tower
Never quite came.

*

The stratifications of love –
Animalcules of heartache,
Vision's foraminifera,
Corals, tiny collects of joy –

Dropping to the silt of selves
In the depths. Suddenly
Continents collide, or
Against the maw of a trough

The land crushes. Mountains
From the drowned strata
Build their arcs.
Volcanoes tear at the sky.

And before erosion tames them
We live among gods –
Himàlaya called 'falling in love',
New skies of an unpredictable weather.

*

Out of the soup of friendships,
Theatricals, mass-going
In the padlocked Welsh sabbath,

Certainties sometimes
Precipitated:
Couples opened their annals.

Civilizations grew
From frankness.
Despair was countenanced.

Margaret – so much in love
Her handwriting changed overnight
To a copy of his –

And he, pulled somehow
Into a commitment against the grain,
Left her to rage, weeks, months,

Against the necessity
To love him. Left her
A kind of widow to his friends.

*

Friendship the Open Sesame
That stumbled me one afternoon
Down to the cave

And in the twenty-four jars
Spilling treasure –
Work like a spider's web,
Diamonds swaying on it
Like tears –
Stoles, chasubles
Stitched with blood drops,
Rubies, sunsets,
Coronets of sapphire,
Dreams of cold faith,
Fidelities, pearls ...

It was a different world I saw then
For those moments

And along the sights of gemstones
Looked with her eyes,
Judged with her heart

Until I reached for the lamp with its genie
And I fell in love.

*

Poor love walked with Dante by the Menai,
The Duecento on the water
Like phosphorescence,
Like fireflies.

Margaret a paradoxical Beatrice
In a manner of widowhood
Unsure, pugnacious,
Twinkling with sorrow ...

I saw with her feeling heart
The starry ones
For the moment
Move in the sky.

The leopard hid in the precipitates
Of his astrology. Poor love
Suffered their certainties
Like a Way of the Cross.

I crawled from *fin' amor*
Like a corpse from a massacre.

Chapter 8. LIZ

... The one who's going to play the lead is the thin girl sitting there silent. Staring in front of her. Thinking. She's thinking that soon she's going to be Antigone. That she'll suddenly stop being the thin dark girl whose family didn't take her seriously, and rise up alone against everyone. Against Creon, her uncle ... the king. She's thinking she's going to die ... though she's still young, and like everyone else would have preferred to live.

But there's nothing to be done. Her name is Antigone, and she's going to have to play her part right through to the end.
(Anouilh: Antigone, trans. Barbara Bray)

At the end, though, is the thin dark girl bereft
So suddenly of her death?

I watched Liz, the flicker of Antigone's dying
Still shameless in her eyes,

Stand above Creon
Who sat defeated, crumpled by her.

I saw the secret ways into the dark
Behind her shining eyes

Opening to me. Antigone's death
A door. Steps into the silence

Needed my voice to cry out –
Call to her ...

Go down to find her.

*

The spillage of tragedy glimmered.
It picked out strength, uncertainty, fear
Like a phosphorescence.

In the ghostlight she was Eve,
She was Andromeda,
She was Cordelia.

I wanted her, would write her
As my creation, give her words
And she fulfil them.

Humbly, I'd to give her dreams,
To dream her into wholeness,
To speak her peace.

> *I'd engage you in my meaning,* I said,
> *As a swan engages its reflection,*
> *Two categories moving as one,*
> *Ignoring mind's priorities.*
>
> *You'd reach out towards me,* I said,
> *See only empty ripples, yet*
> *By that act*
> *Validate relation ...*

In that unknowing I became poet,
I claimed my world.

But it wasn't peace I gave Liz –
Only poor love's excuse
For impotent words.

*

My dark twin
Was it, that enticed me back
Where the foetus grew

In the cracked geology
Of the womb –
Poem after poem?

I hid my head,
My eyes, kneeling
Into a chair

Till the words came,
Till the fairytale
Birth was danced.

> *Liz*, I said, *the poet is the male spirit creating.*
> *The phallus in coition*
> *Must reach out and into*
> *And through, until*
>
> *The fires of the flesh*
> *Are burst open,*
> *And the physical vision*
> *Seeks out the new child.*

But whose dream was it
I was giving Liz –
Healing for her

Or my far-away potency
Entering like a twin
Into her flesh?

*

He was a dervish, a magician.
My twin danced, he fingered with light
The goddess dark.

The leopard was breathless:
Followed with his eyes
As fires smoked and scarred

And the created world
Like a kaleidoscope
Juggled and swerved, vanished, regrouped.

Images of innocence –
A crowding populace, a solitude
Topsy-turvy with love.

Poems that danced for her my birth
Into the light
And broad sky of her peace.

Chapter 9. JANICE

Gerard said, 'Love is like cards.
You have to play your hand
Till you've no more to play.'

Moping poor love was, moping round the town,
Crying like the fifth little pig
'Wee, wee, wee' all the way home ...

Gerard said, 'If you can't play,
You lose.'
Wee, wee, wee

To Jan, to Linda, to Lys,
To Anna captive, flat with a broken back,
To Dick hitchhiking me through Ireland
        to keep me sane –

Wee, wee. wee
To anyone who'd listen –
My bride false. Poor love beaten.

And if you can't play, you lose –
Leopard, for the first time, looking out
Through poor love's eyes.

*

A theology of darkness,
Of sepulchre.

Love beyond love,
Truth beyond truth –
Unhoped for, unloved.

God dead.
In the dark saturday of the world
God dead.
In the dry sepulchre
God.

And you, fool with your cap and bells,
Sitting in the spoil heaps,
Waiting No Thing.

*

World was a sexual tumble
On a slag heap.

In, out.
In, out –

Adverts, drugs,
    Devil, saint,
Predator, prey,
    Frenzy, idleness

Between neon and opium
Between sulphur and salt
Between viper ard frog
Between frenzy and sloth

Between the city and the pit
Between the dark and the dark
Between the ego and sleep
Between stream and stream

In, out,
In, out –

Unreality of particle physics
Unreality of sensory experience

In the land where tides sweep over and over
In the tidal country of proton and neutron
In the long equilibria of strangeness
In the dark vortices of the velocity of light

En una noch' oscura
(And in which darkness, which obscurity of night?)
In this buried land of Cantre'r Gwaelod
Where catfish glide down the aisles of churches

In, out,
In, out –

Coming, coming

In this buried land
One dark night
With my love's anxieties flaming within me
Like an implosion of sunlight, and no one to notice,

Alone, with the sea-gates wide open behind me,
I left my home in the better-class suburbs of death
And went out.
                    I had finished.

A wet dream.
A far away potency
Receding like the Red Shift.

Leviathan munches my bones as the coral and pearl
Elegance of dawn touches the surfaces
Of lake and rockface, ocean
And tumultuous streams.

*

The leopard walked in the veld.
So far from the trees
And mightily afraid
He growled piteously to himself.

A pride of lion rumbled like thunder.
He started to trot, to gallop.
Ah, at last! A watercourse
And the beginning of forest.

'Ho, Catullus,' he cried in surprise,
'What are you doing here?
This isn't Italy, is it? Or Sirmio
These holms, Lake Garda's almost island?'

'Hush,' said Catullus, his face
Twisted with fear. 'This is Phrygia. Look.'
And the leopard crouched with him
Watching the steep white strand, the pinetrees.

Suddenly a boat skimmed the breakers,
Grounded on shingle. Eagerly
Like a boy, the sailor leapt to land.
He looked up. I saw it was poor love.

He looked down. The hangers between his thighs
He sliced off. With a sharp chipped flint
He cut. I saw its eyes
In holy ecstasy, light

On the drops of new blood. 'Ho, friends,' it cried,
'Let us run, beat drum, pipe, sing loud
In the forest, in the Goddess dark.
Cybele, mother ...' Words lost in the trees.

Like a school let out, hullabaloo
Crowded the world. Catullus, ashen-lipped,
Whispered, 'This was an Athenian,
A warrior, loved by its family, its father's son.

Look, its children, its inheritors
Never now born.' The leopard stared at him.
Poor love was out there, shouting in the trees.
Then silence. 'He regrets it now,'

Catullus said, 'but no, the Mother
Will not let him. She sends her messenger.'
A huge bearded lion, with narrowing eyes
Cut off its path to the sea.

Piteously it fled to the forests of childhood.
Racket of pipes, flutes, drums
And the ululation of boys' voices
Countered the lion's roar, the growl of breakers.

Darkness. Then dawn again. 'Look,' said Catullus –
Suddenly a boat skimmed the breakers,
Grounded on shingle. Eagerly
Like a boy, poor love leapt to land ...

★

A lion is my father, I said,
And for thirty years
I have not spoken with him.

In the middle of a sentence
Hysteria took hold of me.
I'd run screaming into the trees.

I never noticed.
How was it
I never noticed?

Gerard woke me saying,
'If you can't play,
You lose.'

It was the ego of a child they gave me.
Poor love cut off its balls
Rather than fend like a man.

I send for my father.
I admit to him he was right.
Thirty years' love spills out between us.

Thirty years' joy
Rings round my hermitage
As I toddle to manhood.

TWO

Scherzo

Chapter 10. ABROAD AND BACK

Like Mole in *Wind in the Willows*,
Stumbling out of hibernation
Into ...

Barcelona, Europe, airports. Expatriates muttering
New horrors of the gardia civil.
The friendly traffic cop marooned
In a sea of bottles
For Epiphany ...

Walking the white streets – will they bite,
These dogs? What if a Catalan
Accosts me? – seeing for the first time
A mediterranean flora ...

Window boxes pricked out, sedate
On the balconies. Maidenhair
Sprouting from grids. Along the tramways
Oranges
On dusty trees
Gleamed like adverts.

*

The sad Catalan dramatist came to lunch.
'It was actually illegal, till six months ago,
To have performances. Police
Broke them up, even in private ...'
He couldn't believe Wesker was box-office.

I went by funicular railway where Franco
Had endowed a convent perpetually to intercede
For the sins of the Civil War.
Blank walls shut out Barcelona below it.

The city fathers
Licensed a huge funfair
To surround it and pillow
Prayer
With raucous dreams ...

*

I return link by link along the iron chains of memory to the city which we inhabited so briefly together: the city which used us as its flora – precipitated in us conflicts which were hers and which we mistook for our own ...

(Lawrence Durrell: *Justine*)

Bangor? – a city
By courtesy of a toy bishop
In his papier maché palace.

Its sixteen thousand
Would have been enough
For a fifth-century polis

And in modern terms, too,
Strut differently
To the mere towns around it.

Bangor lads
Wear city gutterals
As shibboleths, badges of power.

It did not grow
Round military or spa or market.
Bangor accumulated itself from bits:

Hirael, Garth, Glanadda –
Old hamlets subsumed as suburbs
Like Camberwell, Shepherd's Bush.

And even if you live here
Roots are somewhere else.
Bangor, always, a sump of hopes.

★

Into this proto-city, this secondary jungle
Of small businesses round the ancient *clas*

(A chimney perched on the Provincial Bank
All that's there
Of the archdeaconry where Glyn Dŵr and Percy
Split a kingdom between them
– 'Lye still ye theefe, and heare the lady sing in
Welsh' –)

Into this proto-city
The sixties erupted like a fulfilment.
Colleges suddenly expatriate,
Dylan Bob Dylan, clutter of the global village,
Pop art and marijuana.

The medium is the message
– heare the lady –
And we gathered in Bangor, at the centre of the known world
Raucous with power.

Chapter 11. LESLEY

There was hardly a cloud on Ben Bulben
To decorate like the shadow of gulls
The great scarp in the sunshine. Sea was chopped
Like garlic, the white flesh of the foam
Just showing, a hint of underskirt.

Drumcliff church tower, a tapestry
Embroidering death
In the green and gold fields,
The lapis lazuli sky. To the warm song
Of larks, cabbage whites dotted the i's

Of tombs. Nettles and couch-grass
Raumed as if welcome, though a new grave
Here and there, in the hulks
Shone tidy with its plastic rose.
The ancient carved Cross domesticated

Its own and our future like a sundial,
And by the neat porch to the important grave
A mown sward directed our steps.
On its warm stone a red admiral dawdled.
A large beetle had business to conduct.

And William Yeats recited from the stone
Vibrato as the bee-loud glade,
Chanting with venomous finality
Verses to teach Irish poets their trade –
The ghost of Willie upped and said to me,

'Cast a cold eye
On life, on death.
Horseman, pass by.'

I was in tears, meeting the Old Master

In such a place, with Lesley my girl
Hand in hand, love's tattering wizardry
Through the unkempt stones. Strange
Thirty years after, you can grieve

For a dead public man, you when he died
Being a schoolchild unbeknown to him
Or he to you ... It was the first grief
I'd felt, anger at the dead
Because they'd died, because they died like this.

'Horseman, pass by,' the ghost recited.
I raged at the absurdity,
But it was the 'cold eye' that slapped me down,
Deadened larks, the butterfly warmth,
The sparkle of graves.

William's ghost
Took to ignoring me as I pleaded with him
As though, lèse majesté, I'd spoilt his reading ...

That wasn't the end though. Ghosts
Don't draw rank on you for long. Master
And children, we stood peacefully at last
Watching the slender shadow of clouds
Like gulls, decorate Ben Bulben's scarp.

*

Now, just now,
and without doors,
the moss re-enters old walls.

*

I salute your body
    with its white and brown.
To all hollow places
    be peace and sweetness.
Be fountains in the glades,
    be rest in the dark gullies.
Let the cry of my deer
    be sounded in the meadows.
Let the rock utter white water,
    let the small roedeer
come to drink
    under the trees.

*

And now a hundred kisses ...

So up to the small of your back
    to the shoulders
one and two, and down the soft flesh
    of the top of your arms,

seeking out the spidery blue veins
    and the roads to your fingers
and up again, down to your breasts
    in narrowing circles around them

erecting most tactfully
    the nipples in the process,
and so up your throat to the smile
    you have in your eyes

and your lips
    where finally
my lips will
    rest.

*

We adjure thee by the living uprising of the flesh
    and the welcome it has had within thee

to hasten towards us for festival's sake
    and peace.

Not in any spirit of low complaisance
    but in joy withal, and the surging joy

as in the giving of pebbles to Dwynwen
    where asplenium marinum grows in rock faces

of her island, and the breeze catches us
    kissing in the cold heath ...

As in the walkway of that churchyard under Ben Bulben
    where we gave Yeats a daisy chain

to teach him more manners
    and a warm eye ...

A red rose in my memory,
    O my dear, my darling, my love,

Am thinking cheerfully of peace
    and you,

and your bare body
    in our room.

Chapter 12. POSSESSIONS

The charred pages chip to nothingness
Flake like a hoarding

He geheold tela
fiftig wintra — wæs ða frod cyning,
eald eþel-weard -- oðð æt an ongan
deorcum nihtum, draca ricsian
se ðe on heaum hofe hord beweotode,
stan-beorh steapne; stig under læg
eldum uncuð ....

He held well
fifty winters – was then wise king,
old bro-guard – till
those dark nights a dragon raumed
who high in its home, hoard had watched
in steep stone-barrow; path down to it
lay ages unknown.

⋆

Fifteen winters. A wise fool
Living in rented flats, free
Of all ward save my books, my music.
Twice insouciantly put out
Onto the bare pavement, landlord lorn,
Took up my bed and walked. Many times
Sheltered by friends or prof,
I was good at losing home.
Then, Mr Dalley. A huge pop-eyed
Viola-player who taught English ....
Attic advertised

Next to the pub Belle View and Tŵr Gwyn
The chapel. I crouched in his doorway,
Waited him come from school.
From then on, his stairs were seldom empty.
'Three more damsels,' he'd say,
'I asked if they'd wait. But no.'

Then I found him
Twelve hours dead on the spare-room floor,
His shirt grey with vomit.

So after three days
A caretaker of the lordless house
I had to move again.

*

So it went on. Temporary places
For the wise fool to hold camp,
Lecture biologists on evolution,
Physicists on relativity ... where
Painters sparked their wit
Off Rembrandt, Cézanne;
Girls dropped in with troubles,
Telling their dreams like news;
And my poems slid into the light.

But at last my mother could bear it no longer.
'You must have a house,' she said. Buy somewhere
To call my own, not perpetually
Footloose, without fixed abode.
'Besides,' she said, 'all those books ...
And you've got the furniture
Aunt Minnie left you, and Grandpa's desk.
We'll help you.'

Dutifully
I inspected the high barrows vacant in Garth,
Steep cairns in Penrallt, dolmens

Roosting like roasting hooks
Over Lonpobty. Settled at last
In Frondirion, Glanrafon's
'Gentle breast,' the wise fool
Dragged his deadman's treasure
Whimsically up the secret paths
To the house, thinking
Of poems he would write, eldritch visitants,
Muses ... Curled up
Like next Spring's fern
I slept.

As John Wain put it

'Yours the steep house on the steep hill.
The town clings to the land's short shoulders.'

But the ravager of night,
The worm whose doom's to seek out
Hoards underground and guard them,
Had found my form in the barrows.
Curled in me now, nuzzling my arm.

*

Deadman's treasure. Grandfather Jones
Trundling through Liverpool markets,
A business eye on the brown glamour
Of Chippendale, Sheraton card tables,
Mahogany planked from trees
The like are not now. Great Uncle Owen
Whose stamps were mine. Penny blacks,
A mint twopenny blue, Cape triangles ...
My boyhood had lived in swaps. Hundreds
Changed hands in a night

And from further back
The Conran silver – what's left of it –

Eighteenth century Dublin coffee-pots,
Spoons crested with stags or pelicans,
Gravy-boats, toast-racks.

Deadman's treasure
Once the barrow was mine, nestled down into it
And over the funerals
Waited its dragon.

The wise fool
Was trapped by it, incompetently trying to ward
For the past, protect it
Like a museum. Tricked into guilt
At a corner chipped, an imperfection
In what was perfect.

The great worm
With one weather eye cocked
In the dark
Knew me. I guarded the hoard.

I slept at my peril.

*

stig under læg
eldum uncuð ...

No, but one man knew it, the path
Into the trove. Perhaps a friend
Coming often to the house,
Skilled, generous in art ...
Not many in that hermitage
Knew of philately, one stamp from another
As I as a boy had known. This one did.
Sifting my collection
In his hands, treasure by treasure,

He'd known just what he wanted, sliced them out
And ran to the Strand in London
To get what deal he could. Almost as if
He had some worthy scheme he wanted me to share
But unable to tell me yet, chose to surprise me
Later, when the fruits were ripe ...

He should have known: dragon's gold
Carries a curse, hopes wither with it,
Love grows wry.

The fire-drake
Discovering its loss, pillaged and burnt in me
All a wide countryside. I, wise fool,
Cowered in the rocks.

*

We were all packed and ready to sail
To Norway ...
Helplessly I cried out over the lost pages
'Gone, gone, gone.'
The treasure was stolen.

There was no time.

Ti Norowa', ti Norowa',
A day, a day, and half a day,
Ti Norowa' owre the faem

To Kristiansand,
Most Scandinavian, most modern
Of ports –
Good taste, wide air,
Trinkets of Setesdal silver,

Knitted elks, trolls.
Half my mind open, charmed
By the little bronze deer,
Trot, trot, by the café ...

Half sunk in grief for treasure
I could never use; had hardly glanced at
Over the years.

A tragic chorus
– Friend, cousin, my own thought –
Sang dirges of insurance, the police,
Duty to see wrongdoers
Punished...

Where the dragon
Had swum to Norway
Slimed like an oil slick
Over the foam.

⋆

Therefore,
Wearily coming home,
Three weeks too late,
I reported the theft

And a detective
Duly arrived
To lecture me
On my way of life.

For those paper scraps
Was I prepared to ship a friend, a free spirit
To the likes of him? Van Diemen's Land,

Police courts, prison ...

*

But neither could I persuade myself
That evasion
Was a civic act.
I could not claim insurance

Nor was I rid of the dragon.

A wise fool trembles in the rock –
He waits the old man,
Beowulf, hero
Of my seventy winters
By fjord and dal –
Who must slay the Worm,
Kill and be killed
In this country of me.

Chapter 13. THE PIT

Sic fatur lacrimans ...
Aeneid, VI

At fourteen in the pit, in the mine
At Abertyssog.

The twin gates of sleep: one, rumoured
To be of common horn, gives easy
Passage to true dreams ...

And me and Idris was working. And one time we got lost in the colliery together for a few hours. We wandered into old workings. We was lost for a spell there, me and Idris. We was practically reared by one street next to one another, down ...

And at last we crowd on sail,
Glide under the Euboean coast by Cumae.
Prows are faced seaward, anchors bite
And make fast, and the curved poops
Fringe the litoral.

Our young men
Jump to it. Of my confrères,
Some try the flint veins
For the seeds of fire; others
The wild beasts' covert
Ravish for logs, and point
To water in uncovered rills ...

But my piety is to make for the high summit
Where Apollo waits. The Sybil
In the pit of the years
Is a mare he must break and ride.

*

Blaen Rhymni,
Entrance to the underworld.

There were still mines in the Valley then.
We came to the iron wheel
Between the trees, the turning roulette
Of the Sybil. We asked to go down.
No, it was not permitted. The golden bough
In the hands of a poet
Did not impress. But the colliers
Were coming up from their shift
To the polished air. Three black faces
Grinning like urchins in a king's robes
Posed over the barrier
To be snapped. Later
We saw them, fours and sixes,
Trudge archetypally
The brown lane to their wives.
Two of them waved.

It was seeing a film set –
Big John pushing the swing doors of a saloon
And the whisky
Trundling like a tall tram
Down the bar ...

But they were people like us,
Spick and span from the newly installed
Coal-board baths.
No one sang
'Cwm Rhondda' or 'Llef'.

They tugged their forelocks.
We were tourists in Zion.
We grinned back.

*

Massive the rock's hewn out, a cavern,
A hundred wide mouths, a hundred gates
And as many clanging voices
As the Sybil responds.

We came to the foyer. 'Ask,'
She said. 'Ask. The oracle, look,
The oracle ...' And her voice
Trailed to convulsive silence, her face
Pocked with black tears.

It was time to pay our dues

> ... will begin in one minute. Take your seats,
> Ladies and gentlemen. The performance ...

... to Field Street. We was living in Ramsden Street, below there. He went up to London or somewhere, from the pits like. But we were very friendly up until the poor fellow died. Cancer, I believe ...

And gently my lips spoke. I remembered his question
In the desert of Wales, in the imploding
Emptiness of a dream:

'O what is coal
That so much blood should be upon it?'

And as I cried, like the pack of cards in *Alice*,
The whole caboodle –

Pictures – soup kitchens
The standing wheel – sunned colliers
Country lanes
Swans – pigeons – ponies put to grass
Fiddles – jazz bands

Federation
Old women tearful in bare kitchens
Hymns – hallelujas –

Fell
Crashing at my feet.
'This way,' said the ghost

Till by the portals of sleep
We halted. The second gate
Gleamed in the emptying dusk,
Was elephant ivory. Through it
The lord of Shadows sends to the air
False dreams.

Father Idris pushes me through.
I clamber out. Rejoin my confrères
At the campfire waiting the day.

Chapter 14. 1979

For thirty years the hag Money
Was kept in purdah. She lived down alleys.
Her children swanking it, yes,
Like naughty boys on the fringes
Of a fairground. Ma Money
Had plenty to give them.

Riches
Were a subculture, we pretended,
Like yoga or Jewishness. Public services
– Air, sunlight, death – were for all.
Money's children queued for the doctor
Like everyone else. Or if they did not,
No-one noticed. Gossip
Was the province they occupied,
An Ulster with normal Britishness
Temporarily in abeyance.

North Sea oil
Flared on the Scotch horizon. Ma Money
Took to fostering bright kids
– Not in her class, mind – while old ladies,
Retired bee-keepers, gentle painters
Like Cullimore, cried in anguish
That we Brits were going soft –
Everything done for us. Enterprise dead.
The three R's and the Eleven Plus
Were cried for in Middle England.

Ma Money was seen buying lipstick,
Licking her chops.

*

Leafless scrub and grey thorns
With hardly a yellow face peeping
From the gorse. A rough sky
And the straits smoky with storm.

I was a wild thing,
I had no roots in the world.
Like a beggar, my one claim
Was the kindliness.

Folk had rights. They stood in their orders
Like a graduation. On parade
The hag Money looked over
Her recruits.

Sergeant-Major was explaining –
Too much dead wood. Grey twigs
With hardly a gold face showing.
You can't run a country like that!

Folk had rights – though as for me
I was a wild thing and hiding
As far as possible.
They found me. Pushed me

Gently enough, on to the square
Where the big men
Untidily stood.
I tried not to look furtive.

The hag Money addressed us.
Like the smoke of white water
She broke despondency and fear
Amongst us.

She weeded our hearts.
It was like Dachau, Buchanwald.
I was a cloned Jew boy
In my star of David.

Folk had rights. Some of the big men
Agreed with her.
Children of the Hag
Handed our gossip to us.

★

Ah, the sweetness of Ma Money then!
She was a real mother to us,
Proud of her boys. Bangor now
(Minus our salaries)
Might survive. She'd see to it
We would not starve.

And I walked in the wide wilderness.

Suddenly the desert was blooming.
The Hag's children were having a festival,
Red and yellow adverts everywhere,
Bank loans, lottery tickets, prize lists –

All the best package deals
To a liberal education ...

Nobody talked anymore.

Ventriloquists of the Hag
Handled our gossip for us.

*

Well, I had babies to delight
And frighten me.

Suddenly in the forum pomped
The hag Caesar crowned with laurels.
Eagles trundled to the last Imperialist War.
Falklands, albatross roads,
Marched them to glory.

We were in Galway then. Wary paudeens
Kept their usual distance.
I could hardly credit it.

But coming home
Under Caernarfon walls
Where empire began

(O castle my mother, womb
Of the aspiration in me,
To what springtime do you bear me?)

I saw the warmongering populace of England
Crowd on sail

As if it were normal, dismemberment or death
For queen and country, and not to complain
At the raggedness of hopes, the size of terror –

The hag Money taking the salute
Of the forty-three Welsh corpses
On board the Victory Victory O.

THREE

Slow Movement

Chapter 15. DEATHS

The wise fool trembles in the rocks.

Through this arrow chink
Consternation of centuries
Is jagged as fork lightning.
I stare with the eyes of a young boy.

In the formal verticals of ruin
I am standing. Six corpses
Pull at the roped lightning,
Sail the ship of death
Through the painted sky.
She paws at the horizon
Like a war-horse, readying itself
To charge.

My sight shrivels. I turn to run.
Dreariness reaching
Into that cry in the dawn –

The castle lay white below me like a ribcage

Good for nothing now
But the bone-saw and cleaver ...

*

Wolfsbane. A hooded procession of poisoners
On the high moors, where a declivity
Allows birch. The fingered ones
Stand in the rain, a confabulation
Of late-summer death, sheltering
Like a bus queue. Misty blue faces
Designer-stubbled with white
Are confident of their trade.

Wolfsbane. Monkshood. Nightshade.
And the white-gilled toadstool,
Deathcap. Deathcap. Silencers.
Well, they're not my business. Many, many deaths
Hurry past with hardly a how-d'you-do.
Most leave no messages. I'm not a dealer,
Certainly no drug-baron. No statistician either.

The messages that my particular deaths leave me
Have been like orphans.
Good King Wenceslas, I've taken them in
Only to find them grow
As my troubled children, demanding
I go to hell for them, support them,
LEAVE THEM ALONE.

Death's favoured messages are seed. Alive
As wolfsbane in the declivity
Where birch shelters them, fingering me
With the pale mist of their faces

In the rain
Of late summer.

*

When Vic died,
Tenderness was my chief thought for him,
The bravery of his wit,
His dark paintings,
Fragility and terror that bound him to
Rembrandt and Cézanne
For even they must rot.
The nicotine dance of his fingers
Half an apology, quartering the moon
Across a guitar.
My chief thought was the brother I missed,
The stillness he was hurrying from.

When Paul died,
The civilization of his kindness crashed,
The brute starkness of his insight
Ruinous and maudlin.
My main thought was that I was alive.
I had fought for him, against his own wickedness.
Against the crawling cyclones of drink
I'd fought for him. I'd failed for the usual reasons –
Was I my brother's keeper?
Now my marginal gloss: I was alive.

And when Mike died,
It was his privacy I could not respect.
To die in a car crash, because a fool wasn't looking -
Of all deaths, that one seemed most irrelevant.
I could not look into that hostile privacy
Where his bad luck was,
He, the hospitable, shut his door.

Ah, poor fellows,
Who are we to question the dust-pan and brush,
The generality! Yet, in its nascent
Monatomic power, grief is various

As life. There's no way to predict
The catalysis. Therefore the absurd
Is what counts.
Like Sex his sister, Brother Death
Is his own man among the platitudes.

⋆

And my own death? Like a toddler,
Waiting
At the top of the stairs
With her arms up to be lifted,
Calling down to me, 'Carry you –
Carry you'?

Death, have you always come as what we've loved most?
A dream of young leaf in winter ...
A girl not quite kissed ... a baby ...
Yes, I've carried you, carried you,

Run with you in the three-legged race
Through the meadows of joy.
You are my hilarity, the poem
I quote from,
The single heart's loneliness
Being a tree.

I'm a crooked man now. The crooked mile
I've to walk's not so simple
As going up stairs, not so all or nothing
As kissing a girl. More like hilarity perhaps.

Yes, little death, I'm game. I'll carry you
A long way yet along my crooked mile.
After all, you are my past.
It's not me that wants to lose you.

FOUR

F i n a l e
Dreams of the gods

Chapter 16. THE MORRIGU

Time was escaping me. Plaiting
Of ford waters, over and over,
Ticked in my veins.

Beside the grave mound in Lerga
I waded, like an animal
Bent with wounds. The Morrigu
As a great bird, settled
On a standing stone, croaking,
Flapping her wings. Out of the sky
She'd seen me like carrion
On the red gravel.

The Morrigu sang,

'Warped one,
    Your bones betray you.
The neck pulled wry,
    Nerves choked
Like ditches
    Flooding nothingness
Over wide limbs.
    Fingers
Are blind eyes
    With only
Illusions
    To feel by.

'Your whispering voice
    Strangles you.
Walk
    Throwing yourself
Foot to foot
    Hurtling
Against hard corners.
    Fall,
Lose balance
    For no reason.

'Even the eye
    Forgets its language.
Focus splits
    Sideways, lopsided.
Sometimes a corona
    Of migraines
Like circling rainbows
    Breaks the screen.
You can't sit still
    Because the tensions
Are wounds, spear you
    Like a stitch.'

'I can still work,' I said.
    'My charioteer
Over the plain, still
    Urges his horses.
Vision's not lost,
    Or exploits
In the assemblies
    Of woven words.
I, soldier stock,
    Work
My craft
    In front of the armies.'

'But for how long?' sang
The Morrigu.
'This very night
Atlas
Lets your world
Totter.
Below your twisted
Shoulder
Lung drowns,
Heart plummets.'

'An impeccable warrior,'
I answered,
'All his life dances
Before his death.'
Morrigu laughed,
Wondering at me
In my waltz of bones.
'Impeccable?'
She croaked,
'Then dance!'

Chapter 17. LUGH

Charioteer, what do you see?

I see a solitary man walking.

Where does he walk?

Between the bivouacs, tents
And fires of the soldiers
Where they brag and tell tales.

He walks the no-man's-land towards us
Like a wolf, sniffs the night air
With a maturity of patience.

What kind of a man is he?

A tall man, big-boned
And handsome, with cropped curls
Of yellow hair.

He's a cloak of green linen
And a white shirt
Embroidered with gold.

Charioteer, how is he armed?

I cannot see exactly. Scalpels
Dance in his hand.
A black shield on his shoulder.

It's astonishing ... Yet no one
Notices.
It's as though they can't see him.

No more they can, my young friend,
No more they can.
This is some friendly god.

One of the Immortals
Takes pity on my great distress
Who am alone on this Táin ...

And I was right. The warrior
Came up to me.
'It's a great struggle you have,' said he.

'It isn't very much,' I said.

'Well, but I'll help you now.'

'And who are you?' I asked him.

'I am Lugh,' said he, 'your father
From the dancing world
Under the tumulus at Lerga.'

He offered me choice. To go on
As I was, till the paralysis
Killed me, in my bones' weariness.

Or to trust to the sleep he would give me,
To his quick fingers
And the strength of my heart.

'I see the top vertebra, Atlas,
Clogged with scars,
Cannot shoulder his world.

The nerve's throttled, frayed
Like an old rope.
I can release it.

Not difficult to open,
Cut through the scars
To the bare bone.

Not difficult,' he said. But the contorted
Bones had eroded me.
Lung and heart might not suffice.

There was one chance in five, he said,
That the sleep would kill me.
I would die at his hands.

He could not cure me. But to release
The blocked spine from silt
Might stop me drowning.

O yes, he had brought me gold
And silver to set me free ...
To save my body from the cold clay ground
And my neck from the high gallows tree.

'You choose,' he said.
'I give you a week. I'll be back then
To respect your choice.'

And in the clatter of wheelchairs, the god
disappeared.

Chapter 18: THROUGH A GLASS DARKLY

He was platypus in the Darling river
Floating on his back like a dead dog
On to the mudbanks. He half-remembered
A panic of floodwater too huge
For his paddles, confusion
In the choking water
As a squid gripped
At the heart, wounded his neck.

Poor platypus snuffled through duckbill
The damp, foetid oxygen
Of the mud. His mask slipped,
He remembered who he was. A faraway
Voice like a tin soldier's
Echoed in his consciousness:

'Well, I'm still dancing,' I said.

Platypus slept, and they fed him,
And he slept.

*

It was a separation chamber, like a still.
Outside, in the anteroom,
Anxiety
Was concentrated out, and scooped
Like scum at a jam-making.
People behaved like ghosts –
Clattering repetitions of worry

Platypus, because the oxygen-mask felt like a duck's bill.

On the dark escalators.
Give a penny to the boatman, old soul,
And he'll ferry you to grief ...

But inside, all was a womb. Hope
If it existed, was purified
To an elixir
Like calf's foot jelly.

Platypus, lying so small under the sheets,
Listened for time's contorted voices
To tell me they were glad.

*

I was wanting to look through.

Solid bodies looming
Into the mist
Had lives beyond the Darling.

Platypus questioned them
Between sleep
As they spooned food,
Tidied him up.

He learned
Something of their priorities.
Tasted in his cocoon
Like sharp rain

The windy streets
Of Fazakerly and Bootle.

★

Casually, 'Oh, I play
Jazz guitar.'

'With a band?'

'Friends, you know.'

'Electric?'

'Yes, sometimes.'

'Sometimes not, then? Like Django ...'

Laughing, his hand
Reached over imaginary
Strings, two fingers
Bent under.

'No, not quite.'

And this otherworld Orfeo
Pushed a pill up my anus –

First he played da notes o noy
Scowan erla gray
Dan he played da notes o joy
For gettar kangra norla

An dan he played da good old gabber reel
Scowan erla gray
Which might a made a sick heart heal
For gettar kangra norla –

And then, a night's painlessness
Under my bleeping heart.

*

Back to the wards, and wide windows of
Openness. I had come from here
The morning before I was platypus.

I had been weighed here. Had my pre-op
Capsule. Had waited
For the call to trundle me
To the knives of the god.

Lesley had been with me, Nyf*
Of the honey-coloured hair.
I was grafted into her worry.

I might never have seen her again –
Her nicknames for everyone
Like a splash of warm water.

We had come to No Name.

Now, in the openness of the wards,
I watched for my visitor
To tell platypus who I was.

*

She gave me communion.

'Youth may weaken,' she said,
'A warrior utterly fail.

* Pronounce to rhyme with sleeve.

'But they that trust in God
Shall soar on their wings
Like eagles.

    There now,' she said,
Looking at me
Warped on the bed,
'Isn't that a wonderful thing?'

I agreed that it was.

Platypus spread his flippers to dry
In the mild sun
Like a shag his wings.

Chapter 19. THE SUMMONS

And the god walked by the Darling
Between the curraghs hauled up
Above the mud, each with its
Fisherman spreadeagled in it,
Dozing or mending his nets. 'Come,'
Called the god to this one, and Liam
Went with him. 'Come,' said the god,
And Karl untackled himself
And followed ...

            But that one
The Jesu did not wake. And this one
(Though he caught his eye)
He said nothing to and passed.

Platypus was on tiptoe to watch him.

Suddenly it looked as though thousands
Of the sick were round him
Humming like bees to be noticed,
To be fed at his honeypot
And live.

        'Ho, Jesu,' Platypus called out ...

The god disappeared. I saw Karl
Edging around the crowd. I saw Liam
Climbing the hill.

            The voices of the Elohim
Sang on the waters:
'Blessed are they that mourn,'
God said.

        'Wait for me,' I shouted –

On Sunday morning
As they walked out to grieve
At his empty tomb.

Chapter 20. THE COURT TOMB

A tomb like a theatre,
A low ringwork, punctuated
With uprights. A court.
Two derelict chambers

Semi-detached, to lie in state.
But the dead, though they'd
Domiciled once,
Bone or ghost, had left.

Platypus trod carefully. The infill
Of rocks in the kerb
Were creviced and sharp.
If you tripped, they could damage you.

In this tomb
Or stone theatre
At Creevykeel, burnt bones
Had to learn to sprout.

Agriculture
Sang its first John Barleycorn –
A new vision of death
From the sprouting soil.

Not the animal spirits
That hunters placate
In the Dreaming
Between worlds,

But unfleshed skeletons
Baled from stone barns
To conceive, sprout, blow
On the windy plains –

The ghostly harvest
Of bones
That danced
Like ripe wheat.

*

And later

Platypus and his children
Built a tomb on Sligo strand.
Damp megaliths coughed
In the wind. No one
Seemed to belong.

We busied ourselves
Copying
With flat pebbles
And rocks the Tomb
At Creevykeel. A toy court
For immortals to dance.

My daughters posed waywardly
For a photo.
A ripple of life passed through them
Like a breeze through grass.

*

The night nurses come into the ward,
Checking us out, temperature,
Oxygen levels, discomfort ...

Hey, I say, you're not from round here.

'I live in Garston.'

But originally?

'You can tell I'm Irish.'

What part?

'Sligo, then.'

County or town?

'My parents live on Strand Road
About a mile from town ...'

She could have been posting a letter
Or even glanced from a window
And seen the toy Tomb I'd built ...

Even seen Marged point a toe
And Alys stand, fair-haired as barley –

Ann Thomas from Sligo,
Witness of an empty grave.

NOTES

Chapter 1 (p. 2). The Leopard. I had a happy, very free boyhood, with the run of Colwyn Bay and the surrounding countryside to wander in, by myself or with my mates. It was wartime, and our imagination was rife with epic struggles and Arthur Ransome children in a world where adults were 'natives' and in any case largely female. That's the Leopard side. On the other hand, I'd been born in India with cerebral palsy and my mother had to bring me home to be reared by my grandparents in Liverpool and Colwyn Bay. My mother and father came home 'on leave' three or four months at a time – that is, until the war stopped them. I did not see my father from when I was six till it ended in '45. My grandparents gave me all the love in the world but hardly prepared me to be an adult among adults. With people older than myself I became the 'poor love' that they seemed happy to have around.

Chapter 2 (p. 7). Unfinished Symphony. My boyhood was far more science-oriented than artistic so Schubert's 'Unfinished' was an important milestone. See the Note to Chapter 6. 'Quod visum placet' – that which delights when it has been seen - is Thomas Aquinus's definition of the beautiful.

Chapter 4 (p. 12). Fresher. When they came back, my parents eventually sorted my education out (after I'd attended five very different private schools) and I was allowed into Colwyn Bay Grammar and finally into Bangor's University College of North Wales where I graduated in 1953.

Hermit and Twin. Bangor was wonderful. In my first year I knew hardly anyone, but I discovered Christianity, read all the Elizabethan poets and Plato's Republic, and wrote my first real poems. *What brings you here so late?* is not only about the Leopard and poor love having to give way to my search for maturity as an adult. It is also a religious poem, about looking for God; and thirdly, though this sense is not so clear, it is about 'my poetry story' and how 'in the Goddess dark' I find poems. The Hermit and the Twin – my intellectual and poetic development – are just as important, even in this first movement, as the Leopard and poor love.

Chapter 5 (p. 15). Speech. My speech-therapist's 'friend who writes' was the Anglo-Welsh poet Lynette Roberts. My therapist later took me to visit her in her caravan and baby-sat Lynette's two children while we talked. It was the first time I'd met a published poet.

Chapter 6 (p. 17). Chemistry. . This chapter starts as a flashback. As a boy I was much more interested in science than in literature or art – even today I generally find articles on taxonomy or valency theory much more inviting than novels. Inorganic Chemistry at the age of twelve was the love of my life. The orderly and seemingly eternal sequence of the ninety-two elements when I finally discovered them arranged in the columns of the Periodic Table was the first (and certainly the clearest) religious apprehension I have ever had. I have met scientists since who have confessed to me the same delight and wonder – there is no God but the elements and Mendeléef was their prophet. I did not know I was out of date. It was

Hiroshima that showed me that the elements too were vulnerable. Nothing in the universe was beyond the reach of time.

pp. 20-22. Euripides' *Alcestis* and Plato's *Republic* were set books in my first year at college.

Chapter 7 (p. 23). Margaret. As a fresher in Bangor the Twin and the Hermit co-existed equably enough, but as I became first an Anglican and then a Catholic the tension between the Goddess-driven Twin and an increasingly God-seeking Hermit increased. The three women whose chapters close the first movement incarnate three stages of this struggle. With Margaret in many ways it was a typical Courtly Love situation and I had Dante and other mediaeval poets as paradigms to deal with it. I may have crawled from *fin' amor* 'like a corpse from a massacre' but the experience as a whole certainly increased my religious hunger.

page 23. For the Ascension of Christ, see *Acts*, 1, 9-11. For relevant Gospel sources for the God-cycle, see *John*, 1, 1-14 and 3, 16; etc. I owe this use of the proverbial 'It's the thought that counts' to Ian Gregson's critique of my gift poems.

page 25. Schubertiades were musical parties (what in Welsh might be called a kind of *noson lawen*) given by Schubert and his friends, at which much of his music was first performed. The mis-spelling is meant to suggest epics - *Iliad* or *Dunciad.*

Chapter 8 (p. 29). Liz. Loving Margaret was part of a spiritual process, a not quite completed conversion. She was a friend before I fell in love, and remains so now. Liz, on the other hand, who took the title part in a student production of Anouilh's *Antigone* in 1959, was a classical Muse-figure. She inspired the Twin, the shaping spirit of imagination, to dance for her the poems of innocence in *Metamorphoses.*

Chapter 9 (p. 33). Janice. My obsessional and hysterical reaction to Janice's breaking off our engagement made me realize that it was my fear of growing up that was to blame. This led to a long overdue rapprochement with my father, but behind the hysteria and drama there was also a spiritual shift of focus. I began, in an unregulated sort of way, to practice contemplative prayer, the *via negativa* of the mystics, described as a theology of darkness.

p. 35 'En una noche oscura' ('One dark night') is the beginning of a famous poem by St John of the Cross about mystical experience: 'In a dark night, inflamed by love's desires .. I went out unnoticed ...' Cantre'r Gwaelod, in Welsh legend, was a kingdom drowned by the sea under Cardigan Bay.

page 36. Catullus's 'Attis' (poem 63) is about a man castrating himself as a sacrifice to the Phrygian goddess Cybele. Sirmio on Lake Garda was where Catullus lived.

Chapter 12 (p. 46) Beowulf, 2208-2214. The only surviving MS was damaged by fire. In my 'translation' of *ethel-weard,* I use the Welsh word *bro* – one's native district: there is no equivalent in modern English.

Chapter 14 (page 57). 1979. This chapter has been misread so I hope this note will help. It describes our growing complacency about the Welfare State, our ignoring the dangers of treating the very rich as though they were like pets or naughty children. Ma Money was biding her time. Ma Money is not meant as a portrait of Mrs Thatcher, but remains throughout an allegorical figure, a personification of wealth in monopoly capitalism. Thatcher was actually more like one of the 'bright kids' that Ma Money fostered, who were 'not in her class, mind.' She seemed very petty-bourgeois to me, hating nationalised industry but with a very limited grasp of what Big Business was up to. She let the 'Mayfair set' dismantle British industry, to the point when they were threatening to privatise the armed services; but then, wearing her other hat as Churchillian war-leader, she finally demurred.

However, the emphasis is not on Thatcher but on my reaction to her total rout of the universities. All their claims to be the guardians of liberal education went down like nine-pins.

Chapter 17 (p. 70). 'O yes he had brought me gold' is from the ballad 'The Maid freed from the gallows' (Child 95).

Chapter 18 (p. 73). 'First he played da notes o noy' etc. is from the Shetland ballad 'King Orfeo' (Child 19).

p. 74. Nyf is the proper Welsh form of the Irish Niamh, the woman who took Oisín to Fairyland.

Chapter 19 (p. 76). 'Elohim' is a Hebrew (plural) name for God used in some books of the Old Testament.

Chapters 16 and 17 owe a great deal to *The Táin,* Thomas Kinsella's translation of the Dark Age Irish epic saga, *Táin bó Cuailnge.*